Illumined *by* Oneness

Illumined *by* Oneness

Resources and Reflections from a Multifaith Dialogue on Overcoming Racism

Bahá'ís of the United States
Office of Public Affairs

BAHÁ'Í PUBLISHING
EVANSTON, ILLINOIS

Bahá'í Publishing
1233 Central St., Evanston, IL 60201

 Published 2026
Printed in the United States of America ∞

29 28 27 26 4 3 2

ISBN 978-1-61851-281-9

Cover and book design by Barbara Saar

Contents

Foreword

It was an insightful impulse indeed from the Bahá'í Office of Public Affairs that led to the inaugural convening of a "Dialogue on Faith and Race" that I co-hosted at Catholic University in January of 2017. The idea was to periodically bring together leaders from national religious organizations in an off-the-record setting that could provide, as the initial invitation put it, "a safe space for open, honest, and inspired reflections on the role of the faith community in promoting racial justice and racial unity in the U.S." The initiative quickly took shape as a site of learning, introspection, exchange, and commiseration among colleagues who came from different faith traditions but shared a common commitment to combating racism. The participants brought a great wealth of experience to the enterprise. Our quarterly meetings were not always easy, as we strove to create an atmosphere of honesty in full knowledge that this can sometimes be painful. I, for one, found myself at times humbled by our interchanges and forced to confront some of my own unexamined attitudes and assumptions regarding race.

Over time, though, the Dialogue proved to be a restorative and even liberating antidote to the rigors and frustrations of anti-racism work, as well as a valued source of fellowship.

As the sessions migrated from site to site around DC and new folks joined in, the Dialogue gradually expanded and, at the same time, deepened. It became an important web of mutual uplift during the coronavirus pandemic even as it moved temporarily online. It served as a critical venue for information-sharing, consultation, and emotional connection after the murder of George Floyd further roiled the nation's racial waters. And all the while, it stimulated an ever more intensive collective process of thinking through and engaging with the complex relations between faith and racialization in America.

The key to this process was the series of reflection texts that formed the core of the deliberative method adopted in our meetings. Painstakingly and thoughtfully composed by the Dialogue's facilitators at the Bahá'í Office of Public Affairs, these documents, read aloud by multiple participants, anchored our discussions and fostered constructive channels of inquiry, debate, and practical speculation, in both small groups and plenary sessions. The topics for the papers were carefully selected so as to constitute a "scaffolded" approach to the complex field of issues thrown up by the dialectical relation of race and religion in American society. Taken together, they make up a multifaceted yet cohesive primer for addressing the problems associated with racism, a guide that can be useful for faith communities and beyond. It is therefore a great service to all committed to racial justice and healing that those papers have now been collected and made available in this publication.

The hallmark of a genuine conversation is that it sparks creativity and generates understandings that none of the participants could have come up with on their own. For that to happen, its participants must adopt a posture of deep listening, openness, and willingness to emend their own views. Having accompanied the Dialogue since its inception, I can say that it met those standards. May this collection, infused as it is with the Bahá'í spirit of inclusivity and healing, contribute to expanding the conversation on how to overcome racism to ever greater publics.

William A. Barbieri Jr.
The Catholic University of America, Washington, DC

Introduction

In 2017 the U.S. Bahá'í Office of Public Affairs, in collaboration with the Peace and Justice Studies Program and the Institute for Policy Research and Catholic Studies at the Catholic University of America, began hosting a Dialogue among faith-based actors with the aim of addressing racism. At a time of heightened racial discord in the United States, we convened leaders and representatives from national-level groups in Washington, D.C. in hopes of creating a space for deeper consideration of the role of the faith community in promoting racial justice and unity in this country. Faith groups work to address racism in different ways, such as service, community building, advocacy, and policy. The Dialogue focused primarily on the level of thought, recognizing that though we must change structures and behavior, if we do not also change our thought, we cannot fully address racism.

Because religion has historically shown an unrivaled capacity to unite disparate peoples in a shared sense of identity and purpose, even though at times it has been perverted to divide people against one another with disastrous consequences, the role of faith communities in society is critical. What is more, the faith-based voice may offer distinctive insights and resources for overcoming the gridlock of a national conversation on racism increasingly defined by mistrust, entrenchment, and talking past one another. Although this Dialogue took place primarily among individuals who belong to communities of faith, the hope was that their insights, arising from religious thought and life, would be relevant and resonant in the broader conversations taking place in society beyond religious spaces.

Dialogue participants identified with different racialized and religious groups and had a robust exchange of ideas. But just as important were the relationships they formed and the support they provided each other regarding the challenging work they were all involved with. The aim was to build capacity among participants to engage in what were at times difficult conversations, and to facilitate similar efforts with others. The group learned through experience the importance of creative and constructive responses that can foster understanding and love when tensions arise. For example, once, when a challenging moment that threatened to disrupt the process occurred between two participants, the group decided to visit a few museums together to gain a shared understanding of the diverse narratives that informed the varied experiences of the group. This greatly enriched the Dialogue process, deepening bonds of trust and connection. The group also developed the practice of having a meal together at meetings and starting conversation sessions with an "open forum," a time and opportunity for participants to share what was in their hearts. All these initiatives helped create a distinctive space where, even though individuals were coming together as professionals, their conversations involved and impacted their personal and religious lives. Participants became supports and resources for each other, and through doing the work they built community.

In this spirit of learning, the conversations were framed by a series of discussion papers that the group would read and respond to. The papers were prepared by the Office, building on themes and questions that emerged in the conversations, responding to the evolving discourse on racism in America, and drawing on insights from the teachings of the Bahá'í Faith and the experience of Bahá'í community.

After five years, the Office decided to distill the salient insights from the conversations and explore them with an even larger group at a summit of Dialogue participants and others from their networks. Drawing on the discussion papers, as well as notes from the sessions, a summary document was drafted and refined in consultation with the Dialogue participants. The aim was to articulate a truly multifaith perspective, one based not on the lowest common denominator of ideas, but on a stronger religious and spiritual perspective that resonated with all the participants.

One of the most heartening aspects of the Dialogue was learning that the materials developed were being used by individuals and organizations to create new spaces for conversation on the role of religion and the faith community in eliminating racism at the local level, and to good effect. For example, the discussion papers served as the foundation for an interfaith dialogue in Charlotte, North Carolina and as part of a community conversation series on race in a neighborhood in Southern California. This unexpected but encouraging development demonstrated the broader utility of these materials, further prompting us to make them more widely available.

Thus, as the Office continues engaging the national discourse on overcoming racism, we feel this summary document (see page 13) could be useful to others interested in the role of faith communities in eliminating racism, including those who might want to convene similar discussion spaces. This document can be used as a standalone piece, although we recommend it be used together with the description of discussion parameters and an introductory note—both of which were refined over the course of the Dialogue and are included in this publication. Also included are versions of the original discussion papers, which, in the spirit of the Dialogue, have been further refined for this publication to reflect insights accrued from the Dialogue itself and from the Office's ongoing learning process.[1]

---

1. For instance, a growing number of people have noted a paradox in the work to overcome racism. Clearly this undertaking requires an analysis of the causes and effects of racism, an analysis which commonly employs the concept of "race" and racialized categories. However, the use of the concept and categories reifies a set of spurious notions that were constructed—and continue to serve—as the underpinnings of racism. Hence the paradox. How do we work to address racism without reifying its foundations? As we engage the growing discourse around

As the materials in this book reflect a multifaith voice, an addendum has been included that offers more directly a Bahá'í perspective on eliminating racism in America for those who might be interested.

We offer this book and a related website[2] as a tool to support the arduous, consequential, and sacred work of bringing diverse people together in profound conversation in order to contribute to the evolution of thought and action so necessary for constructive change. We hope this will inspire, support, and encourage anyone who wants to pursue this aim.

---

these questions, our thought and language continue to evolve. At the same time, there are no easy solutions. We have in this publication tried to avoid reifying ways of using the concept of race and racialized categories. At the same time, we continue to use the terms "racial justice" and "race unity" because they capture ways of thinking about overcoming racism that we do not yet have clear alternatives for. We believe a shift in language is a process.

2. https://illuminedbyoneness.org/

Framing the Conversations

The following two documents were developed over the course of the Dialogue to create the conditions for honest and open discussions where participants would feel welcome to share their thoughts and receive the ideas of others with an open mind. We often read and discussed these documents at the beginning of a session to "set the table" for the ensuing conversation. We offer them here, slightly adapted for use by anyone facilitating similar gatherings. The groups can then read and talk about the discussion papers or the document entitled "A Distillation of Insights from the Dialogue, July 2022" that brings together some underlying themes from the Dialogue series.

Introduction and Welcome to a Conversation

In a time of setbacks in the struggle to overcome racism, we hope this conversation will allow deeper consideration of the role of religion and the faith community in promoting racial justice and unity in this country. Because religion has historically shown an unrivaled capacity to unite disparate peoples in a shared sense of identity and purpose as well as to divide them from one another with disastrous consequences, the role of faith communities in society is critical. What is more, the faith-based voice may offer distinctive insights and resources for overcoming the gridlock of a national conversation on race that is increasingly characterized by mistrust, entrenchment, and talking past one another.

This faith-based conversation aims to foster open, honest, and inspired reflections on the role of the faith community in promoting a search for truth and understanding on the path of racial healing and reconciliation in the United States. It is an intimate gathering which does not involve traditional or social media. The discussion will be on a not-for-attribution basis, which we hope will help to foster candor and understanding. It will also be interactive and participatory. We hope that this distinctive space will allow us to take a step back from the current political moment to examine the underlying dynamics of a challenge that long predates—and will no doubt outlast—the circumstances and developments of the present.

We hope for a rich variety of viewpoints in a robust and fruitful exchange. We also hope that this opportunity to exchange thought and experience will contribute to building relationships and stimulating further discussions in the future. As it has with others who have engaged in this conversation, we hope the experience will enrich the work participants do in their own communities and in the wider society.

Discussion Parameters that Guide our Conversations

These conversations will depend on the participants to shape their character, dynamics, and outcomes. In that spirit, we present some points to consider as we engage in these discussions.

Our aim is to explore how we can constructively bring a distinctive faith-based voice to bear on the national discourse on race and racism. To this end, we hope to build shared understanding. Recognizing that within this gathering of faiths and cultures, there is a wealth of knowledge and diverse experience, we strive to approach this complex and often difficult subject with a sincere and humble posture of learning.

The intention is not to compare different religious traditions and theologies or their historical shortcomings or current challenges. Rather, it is to search for common spiritual resources and insights that we can draw on to address the moral and practical challenges before us. Thus, we can use this environment to share with both heart and mind, to speak from our experiences in a spirit of fellowship, love, and compassion.

As mentioned earlier, this discussion is not for attribution, meaning that although participants may share what they have heard in this space, they should not attribute any statements to the individuals who made them. This format is intended to foster candor and understanding.

As this is an interactive and participatory discussion involving many voices, we should strive to ensure that everyone has a chance to contribute and be heard.

Finally, a note on current events: This is a turbulent time marked by anxieties and uncertainties about the future. Still, we hope these discussions provide an opportunity to step back from the immediacy of the political moment, particularly with respect to specific current events and individuals. The issues and challenges we will be discussing long predate the current moment and will persist for many years, so we hope to take the long view, reflect more broadly and deeply, and envision new possibilities together.

A Distillation of Insights from the Dialogue

JULY 2022

In 2022, the participants of the Dialogue took time to reflect on and distill the key insights on the role of religion and faith communities in overcoming racism in the United States that emerged as most meaningful over the previous five years of gathering. The following is the outcome of that process, and—similarly to the discussion papers that follow—it has been used to facilitate dialogue in a variety of settings. While it may not be possible for groups to discuss all the discussion papers, this document encapsulates some of the most salient and resonant ideas from the papers in aggregate and would be a good starting point.

A period of profound reckoning with the legacy of racism has stirred the conscience of our nation and presented an historic opportunity for meaningful change—one in which individuals and communities of faith have unique responsibilities. Religion has historically shown great capacity to unite disparate peoples in a shared sense of identity and purpose but also to divide them from one another with disastrous consequences. Over the past five years, a diverse group of people from different organizations, faith traditions, and racialized backgrounds has been reflecting—through a sustained Dialogue—on how religion can live up to its potential as a force for constructive change. We feel compelled to share some insights and commitments arising from our conversations and invite you to consider their implications for thought and practice within and beyond faith communities.

Religion, when true to its highest spiritual ideals, has the capacity to unite diverse peoples in a sense of shared moral purpose, binding them together in common cause. Thus, people of all faiths have a spiritual obligation to help construct a unified society in which every individual and social group has the opportunity to develop their latent potentialities and thereby contribute to the well-being of all. In this regard, racism constitutes a profound deviation from true morality and the inherent interconnectedness of the human family. It is a blight on human society. How can we contribute to a shared commitment across faith communities to demonstrate our faith in action as a unifying force in society?

Overcoming racism requires change at multiple levels, and, ultimately, lasting social and economic progress requires moral and spiritual transformation. Further, individuals, communities, and institutions all possess both agency and room for advancement in this struggle. Each of these social actors, as well as the relationships among them, must evolve to reflect trust, mutual support, and cooperation. Change must come to hearts and minds; to norms and relations in communities; and to the structures and practices of our institutions. Such changes are mutually dependent and reinforcing. If individuals, communities, and institutions all have agency and room for advancement, what additional capacities does each need to develop to promote racial justice?

The national conversation on race and racism has been characterized by a high degree of mistrust, polarization, and division. Nonetheless, social justice *can* be advanced in unifying and constructive ways that not only accommodate, but value, diversity. Indeed, justice requires universal participation in both creating and benefiting from shared prosperity. Society can be conceived as an interdependent social body in which every individual and group derives its well-being from the well-being of the whole. If we accept this framing, then we can recognize that no individual or group is truly free unless all individuals and groups are free. How can we embrace wider circles of care where every individual and group realizes their latent potential to contribute to the well-being of the entire social body? What implications does this wider embrace have when we seek to address racism and its impact on our economic life, on social cohesion, on the well-being of families, and so on?

Power, when understood as a scarce resource and a means of domination and division, is used to perpetuate racism and other forms of oppression. Such power is hoarded, jealously defended, and susceptible to the corrupting influence of vested interests. Religion raises our awareness of other forms of power, of moral or spiritual powers that can give us the capacity to transform our social worlds. These powers of the human spirit are limitless and accessible to all. They include the power of unified action, the power of love, the power of justice, the power of truth, the power of pure deeds and sacrificial service, and the power of divine assistance and confirmation. Awareness of *these* powers opens transformative possibilities, assures us of our inherent capacity to create new social realities that can supplant the current social order with its competitive and conflictual uses of power. How does this sense of abundance in thinking about power help us overcome the notions of scarcity that perpetuate racial, economic, and environmental injustice?

Race and racism are social constructions that grow partly out of the stories we tell about who we are and where we are going. Currently, in the United States, we have divergent narratives. Some obscure the role of race and racism in the current social order. Others depict race relations as an inescapable power struggle. Faith-based voices have a responsibility to contribute to the emergence of a shared, inclusive, realistic, yet aspirational understanding of the American story—a story that gives meaning to our past and present, orients us to a possible future of shared prosperity, and inspires us to assume our moral responsibilities in the wider community of nations. How can we begin to develop language, concepts, and vision for a better world rather than simply a description of the world as it is? How can these capacities emerge from an awareness of our common humanity and our inherent dignity and nobility, rather than from our current conditions of oppression?

The insights and commitments articulated above constitute an earnest and urgent invitation to explore the role that religion must play in overcoming racism in our society. Participants in the Dialogue hope to learn, alongside all like-minded people, how to translate these insights and commitments into meaningful, effective, transformative conversation and action. Toward this end, you are invited to study this statement with others, reflect on its implications, and join us on this path of learning in action.

Discussion Papers

An Overview of Racism in the United States and a Faith-Based Approach to the Issue

JANUARY 2017

The connections between faith and the struggle for racial justice are manifold and deep. Throughout history, religion has demonstrated an unrivaled capacity to unite disparate peoples in a shared sense of identity and purpose. At the same time, religion, when used for corrupt ends, has shown an equivalent power to foster and amplify divisions based not only on belief but on many dimensions of identity. In the United States, those speaking in religion's name have been responsible for building up and legitimizing false barriers between people, as well as for breaking them down with resolve and sacrifice. In recent decades, as the operation of racism has become more subtle, public discourse has focused on institutional norms and the tension between efforts to change laws and policies versus efforts to change hearts. But religious actors—those concerned both with the individual heart and with the wider society—have certainly never left the conversation, and questions of how individuals and communities of faith can contribute to addressing the personal, social, and structural dimensions of racism continue to be pressing.

Racism in the United States

The United States' long, complex, and tragic history of racism is well known but often insufficiently acknowledged. Centuries of slavery and Jim Crow, of the decimation and marginalization of native populations, and of bigotry toward successive generations of immigrants of all stripes have left deep scars. What is more, despite great strides forward, the bane of racism has proved remarkably resilient, manifesting itself in the twenty-first century in new and less overt ways in U.S. institutions, as well as in the hearts and minds of the American people. It exists, therefore, as both a harmful legacy of the past, whose effects all have inherited, and a shameful reality of the present, in which all live and participate.

In this connection, separateness and disparities of various kinds are the outcome of choices made not only by individuals but also by societal institutions, and the simple fact is that they remain widespread. To offer but a few examples, on average, households categorized as "black" bring in just 61% of the income of households categorized as "white" and have less than 8% of the wealth. The unemployment rate differs significantly between these groups, and studies show that identical job applications submitted by individuals with "African American-sounding" names are less likely to receive a callback than those with "white-sounding names." American cities continue to be divided along racialized lines as a result of the discriminatory housing laws of the past, as well as current practices: People in minoritized groups are offered worse conditions and higher rents, shown fewer apartments, steered to specific neighborhoods, quoted higher interest rates or turned down for conventional mortgage loans, and were more often targeted for subprime loans prior to the financial crisis. The combination of wealth inequality and segregated communities has contributed to stark contrasts in investment and educational outcomes in the nation's property-tax-funded, and still conspicuously-unintegrated, public schools. The effects of racism can be seen in discrepancies in the rates at which different racialized groups become embroiled in the criminal justice system.

In recent years, there has been a growing sense in many quarters that relations along racialized lines are deteriorating. An increasing awareness of violence with clear racial dimensions has occasioned outrage, as well as an upsurge in confrontational approaches to the issue. The fraught national political discourse has brought to the fore and exacerbated deep-seated racial tensions in the form of increasingly extreme rhetoric and fractured and often counterproductive dialogue on race. Finally, sixty years after Martin Luther King Jr. voiced the uncomfortable truth that Sunday morning was the most segregated hour in American life, it is estimated that nearly half of all U.S. congregations still do not have a single member of another racialized group and that a single group comprises more than 80% of the membership in nine out of ten congregations.

A Faith-Based Approach

As these divisions and inequalities are both social and moral issues, it is the duty of people of faith to constructively engage with this subject and to lend their voices to it. This contribution begins with, and is founded on, the belief that the soul has no race or ethnicity and that each person is created equal in dignity and worth. However, it also acknowledges that, though racial categories are socially constructed and are not rooted either in biology or the spirit, racial identity can have a powerful impact on people's lives. Racial prejudice and oppression have not only caused untold suffering, they have also corrupted its perpetrators. Racial categories and racialized thinking affect us all. It is important for all people, and particularly those oriented by an explicit moral framework, to acknowledge these painful truths and affirm that progress will be hindered so long as society does not fully reckon with the evil of racism. Understanding of the spiritual source and dignity of human life impels people of faith to bear witness to their brothers and sisters, to heal their shared humanity, and to forge new bonds of friendship and community between those of all backgrounds.

Religious faith aspires to build fellowship and harmony among all. But racial unity can only be achieved through racial justice, which means neither avoiding nor erasing diversity. Rather, it entails honoring differences and celebrating the beauty of the human family by bringing people together in mutual support and honest striving. It entails seeing difference not as an obstacle but as a boundless source of strength that enriches the social fabric and equips society to better tackle complex problems and build true prosperity. Much like a physical body, whose differentiated cells and organs derive their well-being from the well-being of the whole, an organically interdependent society would work in an integrated and harmonious way, permitting its component parts to fully realize their unique capacities.

Racism, as a multi-faceted system of power and privilege that functions through attitudes and behaviors and through social structures, must be tackled on both the personal and societal levels, in symbol as well as in substance. So long as racism is conceived of purely as a question of personal bigotry, on the one hand, or a problem of unjust institutions, on the other, steps taken to address the problem will only produce superficial change. In this regard, faith groups have a unique perspective and opportunity to move the conversation forward.

As people well familiar with the value of community, whose traditions speak of the connections between individual and collective transformation and who have been charged with the spiritual duty to care for their neighbors and the world around them, people of faith know they must attend to external conditions and social arrangements in order to build justice. At the same time, being fundamentally concerned with the inner life and moral development of the individual and aware that every person has the potential to do both good and evil, they know that a sense of purpose driven only by the desire to change society, with no attention being paid to the need for personal growth and transformation, is easily misdirected; the person who blames society for every wrong and ignores the importance of individual responsibility loses respect and compassion for others and is prone to divisive, antagonistic, or even violent actions in pursuit of social change. Religious systems of belief provide both deep sources of motivation and a bulwark against conceptions of human nature that give unabashed primacy to the ego and self-interest. In their teachings, one finds a foundation for hopefulness, perseverance, altruism, and faith in others.

It is clear, then, that a distinctively faith-based response to racism would be motivated by true empathy, eschew self-righteousness, seek sincere dialogue, be guided by a commitment to justice, and value self-sacrifice over self-satisfaction. It would be directed by a twofold sense of purpose—by the idea that, for lasting progress to be achieved, a project of social change cannot be divorced from a project of individual transformation. This dual purpose would be based on an understanding that, in this struggle, all individuals, communities, and institutions possess both agency and room for advancement.

Toward a Sustained Conversation

It is hoped that, as a first step toward making a contribution to addressing the above challenges, this Dialogue will create an environment in which we can explore together the distinctive moral perspectives and practical proposals that faith-based groups might offer to discourse on overcoming racism in this country. We hope this engagement will allow us to build relationships and bonds of friendship, and that the discussions we have will help to inform and enrich the important work each of us does in our own communities and in the wider society.

Participants are encouraged to discuss the questions below related to the current discourse on racism in the United States and the unique potential of religion to be effectively engaged in this arena.

Discussion Questions:

1. What are the dominant ways of framing the history and impact of racism in popular discourse today? Are there more constructive ways these could be framed?
2. How can we help elevate the discourse on race and racism above the divisive agendas of partisan politics, interest group competition, and contests of power?
3. How can religion motivate people to respond to racism in just, unifying, and constructive ways?
4. How can we create spaces in which people can work through the difficult conversations about race and racism in order to advance together on a path toward racial justice and unity?

Identity

APRIL 2017

Individual and collective identity—our sense of who we are and how we fit into the world—is an important aspect of our socialization as human beings. It is closely tied to our sense of purpose and how we perceive our relationships with others. Throughout history, a significant factor in making social progress has been the demonstrated capacity of human beings to compose identities that go beyond difference.

Yet those who have sought advantage at the expense of others have often invoked real or imagined differences as a means of dividing people—in order to advance their own interests and ambitions. Over time, these distinctions, born of self-interest, have solidified into constructs related to race, ethnicity, nationality, and other physical and social distinctions. These constructs have often been used to define human beings and to divide them into groups.

Narrowly identifying with particular physical or social characteristics and placing these at the center of our understanding of self and the other has had ruinous consequences, whether a particular identity has been used as a basis for seeking preference over others or has congealed in response to the experience of prejudice and oppression. The deeply fragmented social reality that we find around us today is, in part, a consequence of these narrow identity constructs and attachments.

Beyond these fragmented ways that individuals and groups have come to define themselves, men and women of insight, often inspired by the sacred scriptures of the world, have throughout history sought to broaden human consciousness by drawing attention to that which is most essential about human nature: the inner reality with which every human being is born, the reflection of the divine in each of us. This inner reality is something that we all share and is whole within us, as opposed to the labels with which society tags us in the course of our lives.

This primary, overarching human identity, rooted in the reality of the human soul, which has no race, ethnicity, nationality, or other physical or social distinction, can be understood and developed in a manner that simultaneously values the many secondary aspects of human diversity. Through the sense of security that comes from being consciously aware of the underlying spiritual nature one shares with all humanity, it becomes possible for an individual to derive greater joy from, and to value, all the other aspects.

At the collective level, our shared identity, which is spiritual in nature, serves as the basis for regarding humanity as one. Not only does this identity transcend differences of birth or upbringing, but it also inspires action by uniting people and leading them to cooperate, form relationships, and build communities. The principle of the oneness of humankind is an expression of our underlying reality.

An analogy of the human body can illustrate how the principle of oneness can govern social organization. Much like the human body, the interdependent body of humanity is composed of diverse elements whose well-being can only be achieved through integration and coordination. Millions of cells, with an extraordinary diversity of forms and functions, collaborate to make the existence of the human being possible. They give and receive whatever is needed for their individual functioning as well as for the growth and welfare of the whole. No cell or organ lives apart from the human body, and the well-being of each derives from the well-being of the whole. Far from implying a hierarchy of functions, it is the unity and interdependence of the body's diverse cells and organs that permits the full realization of the distinctive capacities inherent in each.

No one would try to explain the life of a healthy body in terms of concepts used so freely to describe society nowadays, such as the concept of self-interested competition for scarce resources. Nor would one argue that in order for a body to function better, all of its cells should become identical; such uniformity would make the body incapable of carrying out any of the complex functions necessary for its existence. The principle that governs the functioning of the human body is unity in diversity. It is possible to conceive of human society in a similar way. Society is composed of myriads of individuals and groups who have various affiliations and secondary identities, but who also have a primary identity, rooted in the spiritual nature that they share with the rest of humanity.

An integral component for the realization of this organic unity among humanity is justice. Justice ensures that every individual and group has the opportunity to develop their full potential in order to contribute to the betterment of society. Justice is the sole means by which unity of thought and action can be achieved and sustained among diverse peoples.

Undeniably, there are groups of people in the world today who are experiencing oppression and whose positive sense of identity is being undermined. The identities of such groups need to be recognized and affirmed. Yet, a mature humanity must go further and recognize the broader identity shared by all in order to overcome the injustices facing so many. Without this recognition, identity-based struggles can become ends in themselves; efforts to raise consciousness and address the conditions of injustice that affect a particular group can lead to reinforcing divisive distinctions; and it will become increasingly difficult to build a society that embodies the principle of the oneness of humanity and is free from the many forms of prejudice and discrimination that afflict the world. Ultimately, humanity must recognize that the shared primary identity that reflects the reality of all human beings forms the basis of their collective efforts to advance the common good.

Discussion Questions:

1. How do we recognize difference without glorifying it, obscuring commonalities, or creating divisions between people?

2. How do we assure that, under the banner of unity, we are not promoting uniformity but, rather, are seeking to create environments of unity that embody justice and value diversity?
3. How do we help people develop their primary identity by taking into consideration their spiritual reality and their connection with others?

Tone, Language, and Posture in Addressing Racism

JULY 2017

> "Do not let kindness and truth leave you; Bind them around your neck, Write them on the tablet of your heart."
>
> —Proverbs 3:3

> "A kindly tongue is the lodestone of the hearts of men. It is the bread of the spirit, it clotheth the words with meaning, it is the fountain of the light of wisdom and understanding."
>
> —Bahá'u'lláh

Our national conversation on race, as with our national conversation on many subjects, has become increasingly defined by mistrust and entrenchment. Across the political and ideological spectrum, leading voices have contented themselves with talking only to their own factions and past one another. Stridency has come to be conflated with seriousness, courtesy with weakness, anger with credibility, and concession with betrayal.

Prizing debate over dialogue, this posture results in a language designed more to win points and satisfy one's own sense of indignation than to build understanding or make progress.

Against this backdrop, people of faith have a unique opportunity to put forward a voice that rises above the din and helps lift the conversation out of its present state of gridlock. Taking as our goal the reshaping of culture based on principles of sincere love and authentic justice, as well as the development of an outlook free of racial prejudice within individual minds and hearts, the question of what values and attitudes to adopt in this enterprise merits deep reflection. While faith-based groups are able to offer distinctive contributions at the level of substance, it is perhaps in the more subtle areas of our posture, tone, and approach that we can uniquely contribute to steering the conversation in more constructive directions. As the voices in our public discourse become increasingly combative, modes of communication that are humble, kind, and genuinely exploratory may offer a chance to step back and look at the challenge anew—a reprieve that many may not even be aware they long for.

Developing new modes of exchange requires change at the levels of both action and thought. In relation to the latter, there are important consequences to the prevailing tendency to view the pursuit of justice as a battle. While there are constructive dimensions of the language of war—including the need for vigilance, discipline, unified action, and self-sacrifice for a higher cause—there are potential pitfalls as well. With religion's decline in influence in the world, the popular understanding of "struggle" seems to have lost more and more of its import for the interior life of the individual, while growing in weight in the social domain. There is less attention to the need to struggle with and master oneself internally, and an increasing emphasis on oppositional struggle between individuals and groups. And in a materialistic culture that glorifies competition and conflict, the dominant mode of struggle often entails the creation of a group which fights for its social issue or vision of society, casting progress as the defeat of one's ideological adversaries.

Such an approach tends to breed resentment, sow the seeds of its own undoing, and foster a pattern of thinking and speaking that divides the social body into losers and winners, good guys and bad guys, those who "get it" and those who don't. Forgotten is the truth, eloquently expressed by Russian author Aleksandr Solzhenitsyn, that "the line dividing good and evil cuts through the heart of every human being." Recognition of this insight inspires deep humility—the knowledge that we are never complete in our understanding or our testimony, and therefore frequently have something to learn from those of a differing perspective. It also induces an inclination to ensure that means are consistent with ends, that, in our desire to build a just and unified society, we do not give way to apparently expedient approaches that are divisive and will ultimately undermine the unity we seek.

At the heart of so much of humanity's religious and moral heritage lies the golden rule: the notion that we should treat others as we ourselves would want to be treated. No doubt this principle for personal conduct has parallels at the level of social discourse—for instance, in the fact that we tend to be more influenced by the honey of a kindly tongue than the vinegar of a pointed argument. While the dominant ways of the world pit justice and compassion against one another, religious teachings reveal their underlying harmony. Either virtue, unmoderated by the other, can become destructive to the individual and society: Justice without compassion results in vindictiveness, and compassion without justice results in destructive permissiveness. Religion owes its very existence to loving educators patiently creating the conditions by which human error could be corrected and divine guidance could be received, understood, and embraced—even when that guidance directly challenged people. This truth testifies to the fact that, for any message to be communicated, both a clear voice and a hearing ear are needed; one is useless without the other.

In approaching the eminently challenging question of how to overcome racism, then, it is important to recognize that the attitudes and language we adopt have a profound impact on the responses we elicit. In the context of the daily, urgent experience of injustice and the stubborn denial of this injustice by many, it is perhaps not surprising that calling others out in judgmental ways has become normalized and that taking others to account is given more attention than reflecting on our own actions. However, while not ignoring the harsh and shameful realities of racism in this country, bringing spiritual resources to bear may allow us to confront the issue more effectively. Wisdom, as a spiritual quality that transcends knowledge, engenders a new sort of exchange—one that appeals to the nobler aspirations of our fellow citizens and that reflects assurance that the vast majority of us sincerely desire justice. An act of truth-telling is amplified by a spirit of sympathy, and a warm invitation to honest soul-searching opens a previously closed door to acknowledgement and contrition. From a spiritual perspective, a drop of kindness goes a long way toward softening the hardened clay impeding recognition, forgiveness, reconciliation, and change. In this connection, one may recall the biblical injunction to be wise as serpents and gentle as doves.

Fifty years ago, Dr. Martin Luther King, Jr.—who, throughout his ministry, emphasized the uniquely generative, redemptive, and transformative power that love has on one's enemies—spoke these words:

> I know that love is ultimately the only answer to mankind's problems. And I'm going to talk about it everywhere I go. I know it isn't popular to talk about it in some circles today. I'm not talking about emotional bosh when I talk about love, I'm talking about a strong, demanding love.... I say to you today, my friends, that you may be able to speak with the tongues of men and angels; you may have the eloquence of articulate speech; but if you have not love, it means nothing.... You may even give your body to be burned and die the death of a martyr, and your spilt blood may be a symbol of honor for generations yet unborn, and thousands may praise you as one of history's greatest heroes; but if you

> have not love, your blood was spilt in vain. What I'm trying to get you to see this morning is that a man may be self-centered in his self-denial, and self-righteous in his self-sacrifice. His generosity may feed his ego, and his piety may feed his pride. So without love, benevolence becomes egotism, and martyrdom becomes spiritual pride.... When our days become dreary with low-hovering clouds of despair, and when our nights become darker than a thousand midnights, let us remember that there is a creative force in this universe, working to pull down the gigantic mountains of evil, a power that is able to make a way out of no way and transform dark yesterdays into bright tomorrows.

To explore these ideas further, it may be helpful to reflect on some questions related to the current discourse on race in the United States and the unique potential of religion to be effectively engaged in this arena.

Discussion Questions:

1. Why is it that talking about overcoming racism in a manner that is kind, humble, and constructive is so challenging?
2. How can religion and spirituality assist people to think and talk about racism in ways that are sober and substantive, yet also loving, humble, kind, elevated, and constructive?
3. How can we, as people of faith, understand the struggle for racial justice in collective rather than oppositional terms and with a view toward justice as a means of building unity?

Racism and Materialism

OCTOBER 2017

We live in a world in which materialism has become increasingly ascendant and corrosive. Through overt and subtle social cues, we are taught that a person's wealth is an indication of his or her worth, that one's physical appearance is of primary importance, that acquisition and consumption is a way of life, and that the measure of a society lies in the degree of its material development and the growth of its economy. These views and values are conveyed in a myriad spoken and unspoken ways, and they operate on us in a complex and insidious manner, affecting our mental and emotional health, our interpersonal relationships, our community dynamics, our laws and policies, and our culture and values. Materialistic conceptions of human existence and human society have also contributed to a rise in instrumentalist thought, as individual and collective activities are judged and valued not on the basis of their intrinsic goodness or rightness, but rather according to their ability to promote economic gain, in some cases benefiting only a few.

These materialistic currents in our society have interacted with racial prejudice in profound and destructive ways, particularly in the United States. Violence against and domination of native peoples, the enslavement of people of African descent and its legacies, and the repression of Asians, Latinos, Middle Easterners, and others were driven in no small part by the desire to control land, natural resources, agriculture, and the means of material production, with an ultimate view toward attaining capital and wealth. And while there has been nominal legal equality since the end of the civil rights movement, material disparities persist. To take but a few examples, there are significant differences among racialized groups in income and wealth, home ownership and equity, and retirement savings.

In short, materialism and racism have reinforced each other for centuries: Materialistic values have encouraged the exercise of power over others to gain economic advantage, while racist ideas and attitudes have served to justify and perpetuate systems designed to promote economic success for a narrow elite. Fifty years ago, Dr. Martin Luther King spoke of the intertwined evils of racism and materialism, the injustice of extremes of wealth and poverty, and the need for a revolution of values, which entailed a shift from a "thing-oriented society to a person-oriented society." Yet today, racialized minorities continue to face economic marginalization, as well as stereotypes and judgments associated with lack of material prosperity.

The fundamental premise of materialism—that the physical and material dimensions of human existence have greater value than all other dimensions—has powerfully influenced conceptions of race, often in imperceptible ways. This is perhaps unsurprising, as modern notions of race, secularism, and capitalism arose at roughly the same historical moment and have interacted with each other in extremely damaging ways in the centuries since—including through racialized conceptions of certain human beings as material goods. Racism is, of course, incredibly complex and multifaceted, but the materialistic dimension of racism is one that is often overlooked and may be ripe for further examination.

In his letter from a Birmingham jail, Dr. King warned against drawing a "strange, un-Biblical distinction between body and soul, between the sacred and the secular." Yet, certain strands of thought, which have gained prominence of late, tend to conceptualize and discuss racial prejudice in terms of the physical, that is, the effects of racism on one's body. While one's bodily integrity, liberty, and safety are undoubtedly of paramount importance, these considerations are often emphasized to the exclusion of the spiritual and emotional dimensions of racial prejudice, which are no less important.

Indeed, the intangible effects of racism on one's spirit and one's psyche—which, in some cases, result from harm to the body—may ultimately be more injurious and longer lasting, particularly as they reverberate through the family and the community. What is more, ignoring the non-material dimensions of racism can prevent us from perceiving the harmful spiritual effects on individuals who harbor racial prejudice, as well as the ways in which our society suffers as a whole when our social institutions and structures do not reflect the spiritual reality of the oneness of humanity.

As people of faith, we understand that humans are not just physical beings who have spiritual experiences; rather, we are fundamentally spiritual beings who pass through a period of physical existence on this earthly plane. We are also aware that we are created in the image and likeness of God, a truth that speaks to our essential spiritual nature and our ability to mirror forth godly attributes, such as love, patience, forgiveness, sacrifice, and resilience.

A spiritually informed view of human existence allows us to understand material wealth as a means for promoting human development and flourishing—both physical and spiritual—not as an end in and of itself. In this view, material means are not inherently bad or evil; rather, if accumulated and used in ways that are just and that promote the prosperity and progress of all, they are both good and necessary. As we are able to move beyond attachment to material things, to measure worth and value in non-material terms and to use the material in service to the moral and the ethical, both materialism and racism will progressively weaken as societal forces.

A spiritual view of the human experience enables us to perceive a dynamic coherence between body and soul, in which the body can be understood as the temple of the soul in this earthly realm. Both body and soul reflect the nobility of their divine creator and are worthy of dignity and respect. In this view, the soul not only feels the effects of what occurs on the material plane, but it can also enable one to transcend the limitations of materialistic conceptions of self and identity. In this way, perpetrators of racism may, over time, come to understand themselves and their fellow human beings in a new light, perceiving the inherent spiritual equality and brotherhood of all people as children of God, and—through the practice of spiritual qualities, including love, humility, truthfulness, and selflessness—learn to translate this truth into reality in the physical world. Likewise, victims of racism may respond with spiritual qualities, including love, forbearance, patience, and grace, which, when actively applied, enable them to overcome hardship and to effect transformation both in themselves and in others. And all of us, regardless of our background or experience, have a role to play in the process and can engage each other in ways that honor and empower our whole selves, so that we can effect truly deep-seated and lasting change in our society.

Discussion Questions:

1. What are some examples of how racism and materialism interact?
2. How, as people of faith, can we think about racism, materialism, and the interactions between them?
3. What are some examples of spiritual resources that people of faith can draw on?
4. As people of faith, can we draw on spiritual resources to address the evils of racism and materialism in just and unifying ways?

The Relationship between Justice and Unity in the Process of Eliminating Racism

FEBRUARY 2018

The quest for justice has become a defining feature of modern society. As populations around the world have sought to overcome oppression in myriad forms, as the global community has embraced notions of universal human rights, and as humanity has gradually awakened to its deep interconnectedness and interdependence, people of every background have increasingly fixed their sights on justice as the aim of individual striving and of social movements.

The yearning for justice has taken on particular significance in the context of racism within the United States. As Americans struggle with the legacy of centuries of racialized subjugation, discrimination, and inequality, and with ongoing abuses, indignities, and marginalization, there is a heightened consciousness of the importance of justice and the need for social change. Yet, dialogue around issues of racism is often fraught, not only due to prejudice and ignorance, but also, to some degree, as a result of dichotomous and fragmented thinking around the ways that we, as society, understand justice and its relationship to unity. People of faith, who hold deep spiritual commitments to both justice and unity, may be able to play a unique role in deepening collective understanding of these issues and elevating discourse around concepts of racial justice and racial unity in America.

At the most fundamental level, the human race is one. This truth is affirmed by religion, which teaches us that we are children of the same God, equal in dignity and rights, and by science, which teaches us that we are a single species, inextricably bound together in one planetary homeland. Throughout history, many individuals and groups have sought advantage over others, sowing division and oppression. Yet, our underlying oneness remains a latent truth of human existence. And as humanity has evolved, materially, socially, and spiritually, it has grown in its ability to manifest this truth in social reality. In some sense, the advancement of civilization can be conceived of as progress toward the unity of humankind. Indeed, if humanity is a single people, with shared interests and aspirations, its well-being can be achieved only through true unity. But true unity is possible only with justice.

It may be helpful at this juncture to give further shape to our conceptions of both justice and unity.

Justice is undoubtedly of paramount importance. It is a cornerstone of all faith traditions, a primary value in every great civilization, and a vital element of the functioning of society. It is a profound and capacious concept that humanity is still seeking to understand and actualize. Justice is also multifaceted, often understood differently in different arenas, such as criminal justice, including retributive and restorative justice; social justice, including economic, environmental, and political justice, and the like. Yet, all expressions of justice, at their root, share core features.

Justice is a spiritual principle, which manifests at both the individual and collective level. At the individual level, it is a faculty of the human soul that enables each person to see things with his or her own eyes, to be free from prejudice and blind adherence to tradition, to distinguish truth from falsehood, to be fair-minded in one's judgment, and to treat others with equity. And each and every human being has the capacity to discern, express, and embody justice in this way. At the collective level, justice promotes concern for the well-being, inclusion, and participation of all, enables groups to overcome perennial tendencies toward manipulation and partisanship, and allows for collective decision-making through participatory and consultative processes that respect the opinions of all and take account of the best interests of all. In a sense, justice is the practical expression of the awareness that, in the achievement of human progress, the interests of the individual and of society are inextricably linked.

Unity is also a deep, challenging, and often misunderstood concept. It may first be helpful to clarify what unity is not: It is not uniformity, nor is it erasure of diverse and intersecting identities. Throughout history, superficial, misguided, and even malicious calls for unity have been used to silence people, to deny lived identities and experiences, and to strengthen the position of those in power. Certainly, none of these efforts are animated by a true spirit of unity, nor do they advance unity in practice.

In a sense, the body of humanity can be likened to a human body, composed of diverse and specialized cells and organs. These parts cannot live apart from the body, and the well-being of each derives from the well-being of the whole. At the same time, the unity and interdependence of the entire body permits the full realization of the distinctive capacities of each member. This organic unity does not, however, imply uniformity, as the diversity of the component members is what enables the body to realize its collective capacity. So it is with human societies, where unity in diversity contributes to prosperity and well-being. Thus, *unity* is a state of collectivity in which each member is valued and contributes; *diversity* is honored as a source of strength and beauty, and the well-being of the part and the well-being of the whole are mutually reinforcing.

With these concepts in mind, it becomes clear that justice and unity go hand in hand. There can be no true unity without justice, as justice is a necessary and integral component of true unity. When justice is present, unity can be established. In a state of unity, the distinctive identities of individuals and groups are recognized and affirmed, and this recognition and affirmation rests on a shared understanding of the broader human identity common to all people. Justice ensures that every individual and group is treated fairly and that all have the opportunity to develop their full potential in order to contribute to the betterment of society. It is the means by which unity of thought and action can be achieved and sustained among diverse peoples. Indeed, the purpose of justice is to achieve unity.

By the same token, justice, if it is to be true to the reality of human oneness, must be pursued in ways that are conducive to the ultimate goal of unity. When justice is framed as oppositional struggle, in which human beings are pitted against one another, it creates division within the human family and denies our underlying oneness. Seeking justice for one individual or group at the expense of another individual or group can tear at the social fabric and hinder the collective and sustainable realization of both justice and unity.

Likewise, when justice is the sole aim of individual or collective efforts and is divorced from considerations of unity, baser emotions, such as vengeance and vindictiveness, may begin to masquerade as justice. Justice is a spiritual quality, and spiritual qualities do not work in isolation, but interact with each other. Thus, justice must be tempered by other spiritual qualities, such as compassion and love—lest the quest for justice itself become oppressive.

For both moral and practical reasons, means must be consistent with ends. In recent years, scholars of social change have begun to confirm that means prefigure ends: The more inclusive and cooperative a movement for justice, the more open and participatory the political structures that ultimately emerge. True justice cannot be achieved through unjust means. In this sense, justice is, like unity, both a goal and an operating principle—and given their interdependence, justice and unity must be pursued together as both means and as ends.

In this connection, we may consider framing the quest for justice not as oppositional or divisive struggle, but rather as collective struggle, in which humanity is engaged together—seeking to overcome ignorance, to transcend the forces of division and destruction, and to establish truth and equity. This is not to say that we cannot oppose certain ideas, structures, and forces that are unjust; we most certainly can and should. But opposing one another as fellow human beings presents a danger: The oppressed may find themselves taking on the characteristics of the oppressor, responding in ways that reproduce the same dynamics of dehumanization and othering that they have suffered. In the struggle for justice, how can we ensure that our means are as pure as our ends and that they model the inclusion and mutuality we are seeking?

There is much to be learned regarding how we can overcome injustice together, inviting others in to join us as coworkers in this struggle and empowering each other to improve ourselves and our society. Indeed, justice demands universal participation, as each of us has the potential to be an agent of change and each of us can take ownership of the struggle to better ourselves and our society. We are all protagonists in a process of learning, growth, discovery, and progress—one that can lead to the ultimate realization of the unity of humanity. And, as we begin to understand justice and unity in harmony with one another, we can imagine a dialectic and iterative process, whereby justice and unity build upon one another to advance civilization.

In the context of an increasingly polarized, difficult, and urgent national conversation on racism, narrow and reductive conceptions of justice often prevail, with justice being conceived of in condemnatory ways. Similarly, unity is often understood in facile ways, either used as a tool to avoid confronting harsh realities or else dismissed out of hand as an irrelevant ideal. Undoubtedly, our society can benefit from a more evolved understanding of justice and unity.

Faith communities can make significant contributions to advancing this understanding, given our deep experience striving for justice and unity in our own communities and in wider society; our awareness of the reciprocal relationship between individuals and society, and the need for transformation of both hearts and minds and social systems; and the nexus between being and doing, as we constantly seek coherence in our thoughts, prayers, attitudes, speech, and actions. In navigating and engaging with a fractious and challenging dialogue on race and racism in America, we may wish to consider how we can offer valuable perspectives that can help to promote more effective and sustainable action to achieve racial justice and racial unity.

Discussion Questions:

1. What are some examples—in our own lives and/or in society—of how justice and unity interact?
2. How do our scriptures and our traditions teach us faith-based conceptions of justice and unity that are expansive and nuanced?
3. What spiritual qualities can we bring to bear in promoting both justice and unity to overcome racism?
4. How can we as people of faith contribute to an evolving understanding of the interdependent and mutually reinforcing relationship between justice and unity?

The Role of the Individual in Eliminating Racism

MAY 2018

Across the country, many people are seeking ways to engage those around them in meaningful and difficult conversations around the topic of racial justice and unity. At the same time, the current polarization in American society makes constructive dialogue and action on issues of racial justice elusive. Even fair-minded individuals who long to free themselves and their society from racism are paralyzed and divided by divergent views, unable to create the unity necessary to advance along the path of constructive change. Humanity's crying need will not be met by a struggle among competing ambitions or by protest against one or another of the countless wrongs afflicting a desperate age. It calls, rather, for a fundamental change of consciousness that the time has come when each human being must accept responsibility for the welfare of the entire human family. This consciousness results from a growing realization of the oneness of humanity—what impacts some of humanity impacts all of humanity.

The oneness of humanity—rooted in the underlying spiritual nature which all human beings share—is far more than a slogan or an abstract and unattainable ideal. It has profound implications for both personal behavior and for the way society is organized—challenging many current assumptions and revolutionizing our conceptions of the relationships that should exist between the individual, society, and its institutions. Awareness of the spiritual reality of human beings carries with it the moral requirement that all be given every opportunity to fulfill their potential and to contribute to the advancement of civilization. The evils of racism and prejudice will be eradicated only by a love that is translated into action, such actions as deliberately going out of our way to befriend all, appreciating the abilities of all, and recreating social structures in a way that allows for the contributions of all. This leads to some challenging questions: What motivates us to befriend all when we have seen our actions met with indifference, apathy, fear, or even hostility? What enables us to maintain a posture of engagement that constructively addresses racism in the midst of a culture characterized by dominance and oppression? How do we recreate social structures when it feels impossible that the current governmental and economic powers would ever allow such change?

Maintaining a posture of constructive engagement in freeing society from racism requires having consistency between belief and practice. Achieving this consistency is no small task. For example: A deep-seated recognition of the oneness of humanity enables us to transcend tendencies toward disunity, isolation, separateness, or competition; an unshakeable conviction in the nobility of human beings, capable of subduing their lower passions and evincing heavenly qualities, should serve to protect against prejudice and paternalism, both of which violate the dignity of people; an immutable belief in justice should guide an endeavor to allocate resources according to the real needs and aspirations of inclusive communities rather than the whims and wishes of a privileged few. In our commitment to uprooting racism and laying the basis for a society that reflects racial justice and unity, we can draw insight and inspiration from the unwavering resolve of people who have been systematically disadvantaged and oppressed throughout the history of the United States.

Historically, many racially oppressed people have drawn on the highest reservoirs of solidarity and collaboration and responded to oppression with constructive resilience, eschewing despair, surrender, resentment, and hate and transcending mere survival, to transform conditions of ignorance, prejudice, and injustice. The strength required for sustained constructive engagement has been manifested not only by those experiencing oppression, but also by many racialized white people in striving to overcome the discomfort that arises from their privilege and constructively channeling the various manifestations of anger and sadness at the injustices that have been perpetrated in their name. Thus, all people have a responsibility to act and do their best to establish racial justice and unity, though we may have differing kinds and degrees of responsibility depending on who we are and how we are situated in society. In this context, one's actions should not be simply a reaction to the actions of others. Rather, action should flow from one's own character and ultimately, as people of faith, from of our relationship with God.

Although people might have different responsibilities to act in establishing racial justice, trust needs to be built in the capacity of others to do the work. Trust is a reciprocal relationship—one must offer it and accept it. Trust requires the telling of truth. Without truth, the full nature of injustice—its effects and the actions needed to end it—become obscured. A commitment to seeking and upholding truth can be aided by two tools: consultation and moderation.

Consultation can serve as a means by which we search for truth in a discourse that is increasingly fractured. Whether concerned with analyzing a specific situation, trying to gain a fuller understanding of a given issue, exploring a possible course of action, or arriving at a decision, consultation may be seen as a collective search for truth. The participants in a consultative process are not interested in exercising power over one another or convincing one another of the validity of their perspectives. Rather, they participate with an understanding that different people see reality from different points of view and as these views are examined and understood, new insights emerge and clarity is gained. Otherwise, stubbornness and persistence in one's views will merely lead to continual conflict and the truth will remain hidden. By seeking consensus and then enacting decisions in unity, a particular course of action may be tested and revised as necessary through a process of collective learning.

Also relevant to such participation is greater appreciation and application of the spiritual quality of moderation. This call for moderation includes, in particular, the manner of speech if a just conclusion is to be achieved. Moderation in this case is not referring to mere compromise, the dilution of truth, or a hypocritical or utopian consensus. It is not the tempering of diverse opinions or the silencing of those with whom we disagree. This moderation demands an end to destructive excesses that have plagued humanity and fomented ceaseless contention and turmoil. Moderation in deliberation and action stands in contrast to the arbitrary imposition of views through power or insistence upon ideological aims, both of which obstruct the search for truth and sow the seeds of continuing injustice. A moderate perspective is a practical and principled standpoint from which one can recognize and adopt valid and insightful ideas, whatever their source, without prejudice. From this perspective, moderation is a means by which virtues are able to balance each other: For example, urgency is balanced by wisdom, mercy is balanced by justice, and truth is balanced by tact.

As people of faith, we are positioned to bring spiritual qualities to bear in a way that helps us to persevere in the reciprocal quest for justice and unity. These qualities include love, humility, forgiveness, self-examination, and joy. We should be careful to neither surrender ourselves to anger or despair nor offer platitudes or shallow prescriptives unsupported by the force of example. Rather, these qualities are best demonstrated with sincerity of word and deed. In this regard, we can learn and grow in capacity over time to help our fellow citizens frame concerns in a way that rises above fissures, to share views in a manner that transcends divisive approaches, and to create and participate in spaces to work together in the quest to enact solutions to the problems that bedevil our nation. In this light, justice is indeed essential to seeing reality with one's own eyes and to identifying the requirements for an equitable society. Unity—forged through consultative processes, including action and reflection—is also essential to achieve the power required for positive social change.

Discussion Questions:

1. It has been observed that people seeking to be agents of change need to be willing to get proximate to injustice. Getting proximate to injustice can be challenging and can often cause us to be exposed to further injustice. How do we equip ourselves to champion the cause of justice even when we experience injustice?
2. To remain forward-looking, dynamic, vibrant, and committed to serving American society in the face of injustice is no small task. What are examples from history where marginalized communities have drawn on the highest reservoirs of solidarity and collaboration and responded to oppression in unifying and constructive ways? What are some of the notable spiritual qualities characteristic of those responses?
3. What motivates us to befriend all when we have seen our actions met with indifference, apathy, fear, or even hostility?

What enables us to maintain a posture of engagement in constructively addressing racism in the midst of a culture characterized by dominance and oppression? How do we recreate social structures when it feels impossible that the current governmental and economic powers would ever allow such change?

4. What experiences have we had where we have been able to have constructive conversations about overcoming racism? What characteristics or qualities outlined in this paper about consultation and/or moderation were present? Were there other things that were present that also led to a constructive outcome?

The Role of the Community in Eliminating Racism

SEPTEMBER 2018

In the previous discussion we explored the role of the individual in addressing racism. Yet individuals are only one of the protagonists in the life of society. They are joined by communities and institutions. For this session, then, we want to look at community and the role it can play in addressing racism.

A community is one of the basic units of society, comprising individuals, families, and other social institutions. In the context of community, individuals can build friendships, form civil associations, and, alongside institutions, develop programs and systems that can create rich patterns of interaction and form the basis of common life. Communities can emerge out of various kinds of association, as, for example, the inhabitants of a small town or neighborhood, the followers of a religion, those associated with the life of an educational establishment, or the members of a profession. And communities often develop shared cultural elements over time. While communities of association take many forms, there is a universal dimension to living in a shared environment with others that makes communities an ideal arena for fostering cooperation and a shared sense of endeavor.

Communities in the United States have been plagued by segregation across racialized and economic lines. Legal limitations placed on where people can live, go to school, and socialize have created distinct life paths for those who have been subject to discriminatory laws, policies, social norms, or associated forms of harassment and violence—especially as a result of racialized distinctions. This has also allowed for racist ideas and notions of "who is deserving of access to resources and who is not" to flourish and take root in the minds of generation after generation. Consequently, it has caused communities of association to organize along racialized lines, diminishing relationships and cooperation across those categories. This relative absence of diverse and inclusive communities has impeded our ability to recognize a shared identity between all human beings. On the contrary, it has nurtured feelings of otherness and estrangement.

Communities are potential spaces for building new capacities, where people can develop the ability to speak to people of diverse backgrounds and experiences, to bridge cultural divides, to analyze historical trends and patterns, and to recognize commonalities. However, segregation has impeded many communities in the United States from achieving these potentialities. As a result, we tend to look either toward individual transformation to cultivate these capacities or toward social structures to enforce them. Developing new collective capacities and fostering mutual commitments through a shared sense of community often requires that people live in proximity to one another so they can work to transcend historical barriers that kept them apart. Indeed, the lack of interracial proximity in many communities across the United States is one of the greatest structural reinforcements of contemporary racism.

When communities see their purpose as contributing their share to the betterment of society as a whole, they can become settings in which powers such as self-sacrifice, generosity, compassion, and the earnest search for truth are multiplied through unified action, where individual will and collective volition are blended, and where a spirit of enterprise is reinforced by a realization of the need for concerted action and a commitment to the common good. In this context, diversity can be recognized as a strength. And from this perspective, healthy communities attend to the equitable development of all their members, channeling resources toward programs and institutions that can nurture the moral, spiritual, intellectual, and physical development of every person. Likewise, in such communities, bonds of trust and fellowship, of camaraderie and cooperation, are strengthened. Local governing bodies, educational institutions, and families all seek to nurture relationships of this quality.

Religious communities have a particular role to play in promoting this conception of communities as protagonists in the betterment of society. Expanding the circle of unity and justice can be understood as the essence of religion. Put more concretely, religious communities realize their potential as communities of practice where spiritual principles and teachings are applied thoughtfully to the life of society, for the benefit of all. Within such communities, a process of capacity building that enables increasing numbers to participate in the transformation of society—while protecting and nurturing all—can be set in motion. Religious communities therefore cannot be satisfied with merely promoting ideals of universal love and compassion. They must come to embody those ideals as communities of practice.

Discussion Questions:

1. Religious communities can serve as inclusive communities of practice. However, they have often been plagued by the type of segregation outlined above. What can religious communities do to address historical segregation and become truly inclusive communities of practice?
2. In some religious communities, there will not likely be a demographic shift in composition. How, then, can homogenous religious communities serve as inclusive communities of practice?
3. How can communities address an acute social need—such as the need to eliminate racism—in ways that are unifying and constructive rather than divisive? How can the principle of the oneness of humanity and commitments to the progress of humanity as a whole inform such efforts on the path toward justice?
4. How can we expand our conception of the communities we participate in to include people of a variety of backgrounds,

despite histories of enforced or chosen segregation? How can communities become venues for learning and, in the process, empowering all people?

5. What are some examples of initiatives that seek to enable the emergence of just and unified communities?

The Role of Institutions in Eliminating Racism

DECEMBER 2018

In our previous two discussions, we have spoken about the role of the individual and the role of community in addressing racism, with an understanding that both have distinct and valuable roles to play. For this session we will be focusing on the role of institutions in addressing racism.

Institutions are created to ensure social order and a functioning society. At the most basic level, institutions create policies, write and uphold laws, offer goods and services, manage access to resources (be they financial, social, or material), and provide skills and training. Institutions serve important functions within the social body, including governing, coordinating, regulating, organizing, and building capacity. Examples of institutions include hospitals, schools, banks, media, government, cultural organizations, and religious institutions. Institutions are structures that have a longevity that individuals do not. Individuals can come and go within institutions, but the structure, function, and identity of institutions often remain the same. Ideally, institutions should be oriented toward serving, as best as possible, the needs of the people whom they represent. This orientation has implications for how society sets up institutions, and how it fosters their development over time.

The reality of institutions in the United States paints a picture often contrary to the ideal sketched above. A brief look at our nation's history shows our institutions valuing the accumulation of wealth, the consolidation of power, and systems that benefit a portion of the population at the expense of another. Many, if not most, of our foundational institutions, erected by a privileged few, sought to formalize and systematize advantage through oppression. This oppression has insinuated itself into the whole social structure of our country. To truly uproot racism and all forms of oppression, the role of institutions in creating and perpetuating that racism and inequality must be acknowledged.

There are no simple formulas for just institutional arrangements and how they interact with the individuals and communities they serve. The diversity of human societies, their ever-increasing complexity, and the growing interdependence of historically distant populations means that institutions must continually evolve. This can only be accomplished if we can overcome the tendencies to idealize existing institutional structures and to uncritically perpetuate them. Instead, we need to approach institutions in a mode of continuous learning. This means we have to be open to reexamining the role and purpose of institutions.

How can we foster institutions that see themselves as instruments for nurturing human potential? How can institutions build the capacity of individuals, harmonize their disparate initiatives, and direct collective effort toward a noble cause? Such questions suggest profound changes in habit and attitude. Institutions so affected would shun any semblance of authoritarianism, creating authentic channels for feedback and criticism to build trust and avoid creating an atmosphere of backbiting and disaffection.

What is implied here in many ways is a radical reimagination of the concept of power. Prevalent concepts of power understood and employed as a means of domination, with the accompanying notions of contest, contention, division and superiority must be left behind. This is not to deny the operation of power: After all, even in cases where the institutions of society have received their mandates through the consent of the people, power is involved in the exercise of authority. But all the processes of an institution should be affected by the powers of the human spirit that every great religious tradition hopes to tap: the power of unity, of love, of humble service, of pure deeds. Associated with power in this sense are words such as *release*, *encourage*, *channel*, *guide*, and *enable*. Power is not a finite entity which is to be seized and jealously guarded; it constitutes a limitless capacity, residing in the human spirit, to transform.

At a practical level, to make this shift, one possibility is to strive to develop certain capacities within institutions. These capacities include the capacity to learn, the capacity to administer justice, the capacity to foster unity, and the capacity for consultative decision-making guided by spiritual principles. When an institution acts as an effective channel of the human spirit, the powers of individuals are stirred and oriented, and the community is afforded the guidance essential for its progress.

Discussion Questions:

1. The paper describes certain values that underpin the functioning of institutions, and which can have a profound effect on the social environment. For example, the accumulation of wealth, consolidation of power, and the promotion of systems that benefit a portion of the population at the expense of another, on the one hand, and serving as instruments for nurturing human potential, as harmonizing individual initiative, directing collective effort toward a noble cause, and as channels of the human spirit, on the other. What are ways in which the values of institutions in the United States shape our environment? Can you identify institutional values that uphold or perpetuate racist habits and practice? Can you identify institutional values that transcend racist habits and practice?
2. The paper names several capacities institutions need to develop in order to meet the needs of the people served by them. What additional capacities do institutions need to develop in order to promote racial justice?
3. Many institutions in the United States have played a continued role in promoting racialized inequities. How can institutions seek to remedy historical or continued racist practices

in their structures? Are there examples of institutions already making efforts in this way?

4. What are examples—contemporary or historical—of when an institution acted as an effective channel of the human spirit, stirred and oriented the powers of individuals and/or offered guidance to a community essential for its progress? What factors enabled the institution to act in this way? How would you articulate the relationship of institutions acting in a way that channels the human spirit to the elimination of racist habits and practices?

The Media System and its Potential to both Reinforce and Challenge Racism

MARCH 2019

During our last session, we talked about the role of institutions in eliminating racism. We discussed that institutions need to be open to reexamining their role and purpose and reflect on their ability to nurture human potential. Today, we are going to consider our media system and its potential to both reinforce and challenge racism in America.

Media entities are crucial institutions of society, sharing information, ideas, and values that shape the way a population conceives of itself. By surveying the broad spectrum of news, entertainment, and social media discourse, we can learn much about ourselves. We might say media act as mirrors of our social reality.

But these mirrors can become distorted. In surveying representations of race in the media, we sometimes see funhouse mirrors that minimize or exaggerate various features of our social reality. Likewise, some mirrors reflect only a dim image of our reality. And some mirrors reflect clearly but narrowly. Thus, even when media strive to serve causes of justice and unity they can, like other institutions of society, embody structural racism.

American mainstream media has historically been culpable of reinforcing racist ideas and chronically overlooking the struggles for justice and equality of racialized groups. Moreover, the journalistic ethics that structure mainstream journalism often reflect the values, views, and interests of people with power and privilege, thereby reinforcing narrow ways of understanding reality.

Despite these chronic shortcomings, the media have also played a significant role challenging racism in America. From abolitionist periodicals, to public-service publications, to the plethora of media produced by diverse groups past and present, there are many examples of courageous and truth-seeking media that challenge systemic racism.

One means of challenging racism that is common to media and to people of faith is the power of narrative. Narratives, or stories, are a primal way human beings structure meaning and seek coherence in their lives. Narratives can convey truths, or falsehoods, in compelling ways. They can foster or erode empathy within and among communities. They simultaneously shape and reflect the ways we understand ourselves and our place in the world.

This is especially true for people of faith. Religious convictions often derive from scriptural narratives. These narratives inform our sense of history, our use of language, our identity, and our perceptions of reality. Media narratives can play similar roles. They don't simply recount a series of facts. They impart meaning, emotion, and normative structure.

Narratives are powerful ways to either reinforce or transcend racism. Narratives shape our understanding not only of "the facts" but also of the meaning we ascribe to those facts and the emotions we attached to them. Media narratives matter.

Discussion Questions:

1. As people of faith, we understand the power of narratives to foster values, create connection, and inform our understanding of who we are and what our place in the world is. How might media narratives about racism be articulated in more unifying, just, and constructive ways? How do they often fall short of these standards?
2. How can the media become more inclusive, not just in their hiring strategies, but in the values and norms that undergird their structures and inform their practices?
3. Conscientious people of faith and media professionals share a commitment to the truth. How should this commitment to truth inform efforts to tell the story of racism in America? Would there be any differences, in this regard, between journalistic narratives and religious narratives?
4. As we try to develop truthful narratives regarding our past and present, what is the relationship between empirical facts, emotional resonance, moral values or spiritual principles, and truth?

5. Should the media try to help America overcome racism, through the way it constructs narratives? Or is the media's role merely to provide disinterested information?

Freedom and Liberation from Racial Oppression

JUNE 2019

At the end of our last session, we touched briefly on the themes of freedom and oppression. We now want to continue that conversation by exploring how we can most effectively struggle for freedom from racism.

Racist attitudes, ideas, policies, and structures appear to flourish in an environment where the freedom to engage in self-interested competition against others is encouraged. If this is true, then overcoming racism may require us to rethink the relationship between freedom and self-interest. Is society merely an arena of self-interested competition for scarce resources? Does freedom simply entail the competitive pursuit of one's wants and needs or the wants and needs of one's group, within such an arena? Or, can society be conceived as an interdependent social body in which every individual and group derives their well-being from the well-being of the whole? If so, should we not be concerned with the freedom of every individual and group to realize their latent potential to contribute to the well-being of the entire social body? If we accept the latter, then we can recognize that no individual or group is truly free unless all individuals and groups are also free.

As people of faith, we can also recognize that true freedom entails following the teachings of God, which liberate us from impulses and appetites of our lower nature and thus enable us to develop our latent spiritual potential. These teachings include principles that govern how to interact with others, including cooperation and harmony between diverse ideas and people, as well as a willingness to sacrifice that which is lower for a higher cause. This is the source of true freedom—the source of human nobility, dignity, and honor.

The struggle for liberation, then, requires us to reflect on two essential questions: Who are we now? And, who do we aspire to become? Reflecting on the first question requires us to understand why myriad expressions of injustice and oppression exist—where they came from, how they evolved, how they function today, and how this limits the freedom of individuals and communities to develop their latent potentialities. Reflecting on the second question requires us to consider the nature of those potentialities and the processes by which they can become manifest.

Developing an adequate understanding of who we are and what we aspire to become may also require development of more adequate language through which we can explore and express these things. For instance, though we need language that deepens our understanding of prevalent relations of power and domination, we also need language that enables us to explore and create the healthy and mature social relations we aspire to bring into being.

Discussion Questions:

1. How might we articulate the relationship between acute forms of oppression, such as racism, and generalized forms of oppression, such as materialism? Can a language of transformative social change encompass both without negating either?
2. Many contemporary social systems embody oppressive structures that have been consolidated over decades or centuries. Certain aspects of the prevailing global market system are one example. Modern life often requires us to participate in such systems, to some degree, for our sustenance, our livelihoods, our education, and so forth. Is it possible to do so without becoming associated, to some degree, with the oppression of others? In this regard, how might a binary "us" versus "them" conception of oppressors and oppressed limit the ways we understand and pursue social justice? How might we move beyond these binary categories as we develop a more nuanced language of transformative social change?
3. How can we begin to develop language, concepts, and vision that enable us to construct the world we want to live in—rather than simply describe or analyze the world we currently live in? How can this emerge from an acknowledgement of our common humanity and our inherent

dignity or nobility, rather than our current conditions of oppression?

4. Thinking beyond the language we employ as we struggle for social change, what is the relationship between the ends we aspire to and the means by which we struggle for those ends?
5. Where can we find examples of people seeking to overcome oppression through constructive means of social transformation? What can we learn from those experiences? Can those experiences be understood in terms of underlying spiritual principles that can be applied more broadly? If so, what might some of those principles be?

Historical Narratives

SEPTEMBER 2019

Race as a concept and racial categories were socially constructed to undergird racism. The way these concepts and categories are understood and lived is shaped by innumerable social factors and forces, many of which have exerted influence over generations.

One of the most powerful of these forces is the stories we tell about our history. Historical narratives are the means by which humanity derives an account and agreement of its past. It is how we establish the meaning of what has come before and how those meanings organize our lives today. History connects us to place, ancestry, culture, time, and to ourselves. It is a powerful way of understanding who we are and our place in society, both as individuals and social groups.

Historical narratives are more than a set of facts occurring across a timeline. They are also an expression of values. In what a history records, emphasizes, orders, and omits, we find not only a sequence of events. We also find an embedded testament of the values held by those who wrote it.

Different accounts of history are governed by different norms and standards that make the account acceptable to those who read it. Often, through complex social and political processes, certain histories take a canonical place in our collective memory. Vast segments of society come to accept a common version of what has occurred during a given period and even accept a common categorization of periods into which history can be divided.

In American society, for example, there is a widespread understanding that slavery ended in 1865 with the passing and ratification of the Thirteenth Amendment. The period that followed is also widely understood as "the Reconstruction era." Here, we may ask, what is the relationship between history and truth? What do we mean by slavery? Did this indeed end in 1865? To what extent did it end? For whom did it end? Was its ending total and complete?

If history is indeed a means for understanding ourselves, two widely shared histories of race in the United States merit reflection and reconsideration as we try to imagine a better future. In one dominant narrative, the role of racism is delegitimized and de-emphasized. In this narrative, slavery and its consequences, though regrettable, are in the past, with little bearing on social reality today. Another narrative, less dominant but still significant, depicts race relations in the United States as an unrelenting power struggle. The logic of this latter history suggests that all advances toward justice have come through contest and strife, whether nonviolent or violent. In this view, those without power must always demand it and seize it from those who have it.

There may be shortcomings to both of these histories. For example, how might these histories reinforce the centrality of "otherness" in our self-understanding? How might they each exclude or obscure aspects of the complex truth about racism in America? How might they each constrain our vision regarding the future of our country?

Religion, at its best, is a source of ennobling values that uplift the human condition and propel the advancement of civilization. How might the history of America be retold, by people of faith, in a way that expresses a conscious commitment to values such as justice and unity? Justice requires us to hold fast to the truth of what has happened in the past and what is happening now, no matter how uncomfortable and painful that truth may be. At the same time, unity requires us to recognize that humanity is one. Race is a spurious schema that has been overlaid on humanity. The soul has no race. Moreover, on this material plane, the well-being of every soul is inseparably bound up with the well-being of every other soul—like the interdependent cells and organs of a single social body.

Through this lens, we might ask, what have our histories neglected? Are there narratives in our past of cooperation and amity across racialized groups that we might point to and learn from? How can these narratives be told alongside, and without negating, the painful and necessary narratives of racism and othering? How prominent a place should each occupy in our histories? How should each be framed and interpreted in relation to the other? Can our vision not encompass both? Can we not render both mutually intelligible? Can we not draw important insights from both?

For people of faith, sacred scripture often expresses itself as the history of a people inspired by a Divine Teacher. Such histories have purpose and direction, moving toward the ever-greater realization of God's will through time.

Discussion Questions:

1. As people of faith, how might our view of history—including American history—shape our view of the present and future?
2. How might we find new ways to tell our history? How might we allow for diverse people to participate in the generation of narratives that inform how we understand history? How might we ensure that the telling of history is not just the domain of a few but is inclusive, real, and accessible to all?
3. Efforts to promote truth and reconciliation can be understood, at least in part, in terms of repair for harm done. How might we repair past harms by deepening the nation's collective understanding of how and why racial categories were constructed, along with the enduring impacts and legacies of racism that have resulted? How might this be approached in a manner that enables us to collectively move beyond "othering" so we can construct a more just social order founded on a consciousness of the oneness of humanity?

Participation

DECEMBER 2019

On March 12, 1967, toward the end of his life, Rev. Dr. Martin Luther King, Jr. spoke to a group of local community organizers at Cardoza High School in the Shaw neighborhood of Washington, D.C. He had one message to the people there: "Prepare to participate" in local activities that would uplift their community. And he wanted those gathered to "tell it wherever you go."

One of the most pressing questions we face as we labor to build a new America that is free of racial prejudice and discrimination is how to continually widen the circle of participation in this work. Such participation is often assumed to include those who visibly signal their commitment to antiracism through a set of prescribed words and actions, while excluding those who do not. It is easy, in this regard, to fall into the conscious or unconscious habit of dividing people into categories such as informed or uninformed, active or inactive, or "with us or against us." While such thinking can arise out of sincere motives, does it produce unintended consequences that need to be examined? For instance, how might such modes of thought undermine efforts to continually widen the circle of participation?

All people have the latent capacity to participate in processes that enhance the dignity and ensure the just treatment of all. Moreover, social change is not a project that one group of people can carry out for another. All must play their part. Justice for all requires the participation of all. In this regard, participation can be conceived of as a continuum on which people can move from less active to more active forms of participation. Conceiving of participation in this way requires recognizing that everyone has the capacity to contribute and that such capacity can be increased over time.

There are, of course, many challenges to overcome in this regard. The most obvious of these include active efforts to incite hate, suspicion, division, and mistrust between individuals and communities of varying backgrounds—along with the unconscious internalization of such patterns of thought over generations. Less obvious are the challenges of overcoming apathy, passivity, and complacency, which are bred by many forces in society today.

This does not imply naïveté in the face of oppressive actors and social forces. It implies finding new ways to struggle for justice within that context. Audre Lorde memorably stated, "The master's tools will never dismantle the master's house." In other words, the attitudes, language, methods, and approaches we use to build more just relationships, patterns of behavior, and social structures, matter. New ways of thinking and acting together are needed, in which all can consider themselves as treading a common path toward the betterment of humanity, no matter their background or the obstacles they face. This requires that we learn how to support one another and advance together, respectful of the knowledge that each one possesses at any given moment and avoiding the tendency to divide people into categories that alienate or discourage.

As we learn to work in these ways—to construct a new house with new tools—we will encounter many more challenges. It is crucial to persevere in the face of everyday tests, difficulties, setbacks, and misunderstandings. Doing so requires a firm conviction that humanity, in all its diversity, is one, and that we can learn how to build a more just social order together. Consciousness of the oneness of humanity helps shatter the distorting looking glass in which such tests, difficulties, setbacks, and misunderstanding can seem insurmountable.

The principle of the oneness of humanity must be the overarching principle that guides our efforts to overcome racism, along with every other form of injustice and oppression that blights human progress. In an interdependent social body, the well-being of every member and every group depends on the well-being of the entire body. However, it is one thing to acknowledge something in principle; it is quite another to embrace it with all of one's heart, and harder still to refashion society in ways that give collective expression to it. The difficult work ahead will require perseverance, inclusiveness, and a humble posture of learning. Individual initiative, collective decision-making and planning, and the execution and assessment of plans must all reflect the conviction that every social group has a unique and vital role to play.

Discussion Questions:

1. How might the ways we engage people encourage or discourage their ability to participate in the construction of a more just social order?
2. How can we participate in constructive processes of social change based on the conscious application of spiritual principles rather than patterns of thought, speech, and action we have inherited from a divisive and unjust social order?
3. Participation goes beyond how we see our own role within processes of social transformation. It includes how we see the role of those who are different from us in countless ways. What responsibility do we have to foster inclusive participation across lines that previously divided us? What does it look like to have faith in the capacity of others to contribute to the construction of a more just social order?
4. There is undoubtedly a role for constructive criticism in processes of social change. Where might the boundaries lie between forms of criticism that invite reflection and change and forms that result in discouragement, alienation, or entrenchment? What spiritual principles might guide and inform expressions of criticism?

The Relationship between Universal and Particular Identities

SEPTEMBER 2020

A question that has been present in our discussions is how to free ourselves of the limiting and often oppressive aspects of racialized identities, created to justify enslavement and colonization centuries ago, while not losing related aspects of our identities that can hold value and enrich society. Spiritual conceptions of identity, often given to humanity by religion, can help us understand the relationship between our universal human identity and our many secondary identities, including our racialized identities. Exploring the relationship between these will be the focus of our discussion today.

The body politic has been likened to the human body: Its well-being and advancement as a whole is best served by the collaborative functioning of its diverse members. In a world becoming more interdependent by the day, the importance of these social ties is clear. Yet, as a result of inherited social hierarchies and divisions, diverse social groups often conceive of their interests separately, rather than as members of one social body. What is needed is profound reassessment of the relationship between our identities and interests.

In this context, the legitimate pride members might feel about advances made by their group, or the power of collective action taken around shared concerns, could be likened to strengthening muscles or increasing lung capacity within the body. These dimensions of human existence are helpful insofar as they work in service of the whole. But to the degree that attachment to limited definitions of "we" undermine collective well-being, they are no longer productive. Without a vision of shared identity and common purpose, we fall into competing ideologies and power struggles. Interest group competition has weakened the cohesion of society itself. Rival conceptions about the primacy of a particular people are peddled to the exclusion of the truth that humanity is on a common journey in which all are protagonists. Consider how radically different such a fragmented conception of human identity is from the one that follows from a recognition of the oneness of humanity. In the latter perspective, the diversity that characterizes the human family, far from contradicting its oneness, endows it with richness. It is through love for all people, and by subordinating lesser loyalties to the best interests of humankind, that the unity of the world can be realized and the infinite expressions of human diversity find their highest fulfilment.

It has become more widely accepted today that if a person cares only about individuals who look like them, to the exclusion of others from their circle of concern, this is a problem.

Yet a more subtle challenge lies at the structural level. Even when diverse people today are committed to the advancement of humanity as a whole, they can be limited by divisive social structures inherited from the past—many of which were constructed in a milieu of identity-based oppression.

From a historical perspective, the capacity to conceptualize humanity as an organically interdependent whole is both recent and quite revolutionary. Our ancestors gradually developed more expansive notions of identity as societies were organized on wider and wider scales. But, by and large, a global vision was not required for societies to advance. Today, human activity in one part of the world can have profound effects in another. If we ignore the reality of our oneness, we do so at our own peril.

Given the historic changes of the past two centuries, it is also not surprising that our social institutions are inadequate to our current needs and challenges. Most were initially established to serve relatively homogeneous populations or populations with oppressive social hierarchies. Clearly, new institutional forms are needed. In addition, social norms that place the advancement of limited constituencies in opposition to the well-being of the whole must be replaced by those that value the progress of both as indivisible and complementary. If we hope for a world that does not pit one group against another, we must practice living in it that way.

Great possibilities to cultivate fellowship and concord are open to religious leaders, communities, and individuals, but these same actors can also incite fear, hatred, and violence by using their influence to stoke the fires of fanaticism and prejudice.

Fostering unity, by harmonizing disparate elements and nurturing in every heart a selfless love for humankind, is something religion can and must contribute to.

Discussion Questions:

1. Human beings think differently from one another. They have different values and beliefs. Too often these differences lead to contention, conflict, injustice, suffering, oppression, and social instability. Our challenge then is to learn to live together, respecting diverse individuals and groups, each with their own perspectives on reality, while cultivating a unity in diversity of thought and action through which progress and a peaceful social order can be fostered. How can we rise to this challenge?
2. How can we create more just institutions that value diversity as a means of achieving shared prosperity?
3. How can religion cultivate fellowship and a selfless love for humankind as the foundations for more just social structures and institutions?
4. It could be said that humanity is currently gripped by a crisis of identity, as various groups struggle to define themselves and their place in the world. How might a vision of a shared identity and common purpose aid in resolving this crisis? And how might this be pursued in a way that doesn't fall back into traditional patterns of competing ideologies and power struggles?

The Distinctive Role Religions Can Play in Efforts to Overcome Racism

DECEMBER 2020

During this session we wanted to explore the distinctive role religions have played, or might play, in efforts to overcome racism in the United States.

Though different communities understand and practice religion in different ways, religion can, at its best, be a unifying force in society. After all, the Latin roots of the word *religion* mean binding people together in unity. Furthermore, by bringing into focus the spiritual dimensions of human existence, religion can orient us toward transcendent truths, encourage us to overcome our basest impulses and develop our latent potentialities, motivate us to apply moral principles to the betterment of humanity, and sustain us through the difficulties we encounter on this path. For many believers, these are among the praiseworthy characteristics of true religion.

And yet, throughout history, ambitious leaders have often invoked religion to foment division and conflict. Religious dogma has been set up against scientific knowledge. Religious scriptures have been interpreted to justify slavery, segregation, patriarchy, caste, and other forms of oppression. And religious institutions or leaders have at times been corrupted in various ways.

Discussion Questions:

1. Against this complex backdrop, how can religious communities assume their highest moral responsibilities, today, to advance the cause of racial justice in the United States?
2. Though we understand and practice religion in different ways, where do our understandings overlap and how can we build on points of agreement in the pursuit of racial justice?
3. What distinctive roles might religious individuals, communities, and institutions play today as champions of racial justice?
4. What capacities do religious individuals, communities, and institutions need to develop to advance this pursuit?

Addenda

A Bahá'í Perspective on Addressing Racism

The inspiration for the Dialogue on Faith and Race was the conviction that religion and communities of faith have important contributions to make to overcoming racism in America. While it must be recognized that racism has been perpetuated in the name of religion, this is a transgression against religious truth. Racial oppression and discrimination run counter to the teachings of love, justice, and other spiritual principles that are shared by the religions of the world, and which inspire large and small efforts to do good for others. Indeed, fostering unity by harmonizing disparate elements of society and nurturing in every heart a selfless love for others are among the primary purposes of religion. Religious individuals, communities, and institutions have made important contributions in the struggle to overcome racism, from early abolitionists to civil rights leaders and backroom workers, to religious service organizations, advocacy groups and more. Fair-minded believers of all kinds share a longing for healing the illness of racism that has weakened our nation since before it was born. This section offers a few reflections on the role of religion and religious communities in overcoming racism from the perspective of the Bahá'í teachings and experiences of the Bahá'í community.

The pivotal principle of the Bahá'í Faith is the oneness of humanity. Its Founder, Bahá'u'lláh, writes, *"Know ye not why We created you all from the same dust? That no one should exalt himself over the other. Ponder at all times in your hearts how ye were created."*[3] While the oneness of humanity is a fundamental truth about reality, the world remains misaligned with this reality, progressing toward it only gradually and painfully. The Bahá'í Faith aims to help create a new social reality that better expresses this spiritual principle through unity in diversity, a just social order, and shared prosperity. Because racism has no place in this process, the American Bahá'í community, since its inception, has had a mission to dismantle its corrosive influence, and its approach has developed over time. As the Universal House of Justice, the governing body of the worldwide Bahá'í community, wrote recently to the American Bahá'ís:

> Racism is a profound deviation from the standard of true morality. It deprives a portion of humanity of the opportunity to cultivate and express the full range of their capability and to live a meaningful and flourishing life, while blighting the progress of the rest of humankind.

3. Bahá'u'lláh, The Hidden Words, Arabic., no. 68.

It cannot be rooted out by contest and conflict. It must be supplanted by the establishment of just relationships among individuals, communities, and institutions of society that will uplift all and will not designate anyone as "other." The change required is not merely social and economic, but above all moral and spiritual.

. . . your nation's history reveals that any significant progress toward racial equality has invariably been met by countervailing processes, overt or covert, that served to undermine the advances achieved and to reconstitute the forces of oppression by other means. Thus, whatever the immediate outcome of contemporary events, you need not be deterred, for you are cognizant of the "long and thorny road, beset with pitfalls" . . . that still lies ahead. Your commitment to tread this road with determination and insight, drawing upon what you have learned in recent years about translating Bahá'u'lláh's teachings into reality, will have to be sustained until the time . . . when you will have contributed your decisive share to the eradication of racial prejudice from the fabric of your nation.[4]

4. The Universal House of Justice, message addressed to the Bahá'ís of the United States, dated 22 July 2020, pp. 2, 1.

The American Bahá'í community has been working to apply the teachings of the Faith since its formation during the time of segregation.[5] Bahá'ís have striven to eradicate racism from their own hearts and minds as individuals; to raise children who are free from prejudice; to build patterns of community life that are havens for all in which racism finds no place; and to promote racial amity in society at large, alongside so many others working toward the same aims. The Bahá'í community cannot claim to have all the answers, but it is learning about how to engender the transformation that is needed at the individual and collective levels.

And yet, it is not enough to assume that the current structures of society are otherwise sound and that racial prejudice can simply be removed while everything else remains unchanged. What is required is both internal and external change—the deliberate creation of a social order free not only from racism but also from every form of exclusion and oppression. Such a reality would reflect the teachings shared by all religions: that we are to love one another and manifest the light of God in both our personal lives and our collective endeavors.

As the Bahá'í community develops, it is growing in its capacity to contribute to the life of society by putting the teachings of Bahá'u'lláh into practice. It is learning to play its part in a process of social change impelled by the forces of history and the work of many like-minded groups. The Bahá'í approach is

5. https://bahaiworld.bahai.org/library/the-bahai-response-to-racial-injustice-and-pursuit-of-racial-unity/.

to foster constructive agency, and build new patterns of social interaction, and new ways of working together for shared well-being, amidst the crises and suffering of our current reality. Thus, the work of the Bahá'ís is directed toward building the capacity of individuals, families, neighborhoods, communities, and ultimately entire populations to promote their own and society's material and spiritual advancement. Arising as a protagonist in such an endeavor requires a moral and spiritual vivification, at the heart of which is love, and which is expressed at both the individual and collective levels. Racism, which is so harmful to all of society, is addressed both directly and indirectly in this process.

Foundational to the work of the Bahá'í community is a grassroots movement of empowerment and community building. Through educational activities for children, youth, and adults, the community is learning about raising up a new kind of social actor, one that sees their own well-being in the spiritual and material prosperity of those around them and in society as a whole. In these activities, all are welcome and viewed as potential protagonists. Without the imposition of doctrine, these activities encourage substantive and participatory engagement with the Word of God, which inspires and informs action.

The movement inevitably gives rise to new patterns of community life and culture that encourage agency, reciprocity, justice, and bonds of genuine friendship. And it includes the building of structures that support processes of social transformation and channel individual initiative toward that end. This work is ongoing in a wide range of localities across the globe, from rural villages to urban centers. As it advances, the individual, institutional, and community capacity that is built to serve the spiritual and intellectual needs of communities can gradually be applied to address the social and economic needs and aspirations of communities. Further, the Bahá'í community is seeking to contribute to the evolution of thought in areas concerned with the well-being of society at various levels.

The generative power of this process comes from love, *"love originating from the relationship with the divine, love ablaze among members of a community, love extended without restriction to every human being. This divine love, ignited by the Word of God, is disseminated by enkindled souls through intimate conversations that create new susceptibilities in human hearts, open minds to moral persuasion, and loosen the hold of biased norms and social systems so that they can gradually take on a new form in keeping with the requirements of humanity's age of maturity."*[6]

In essence, the process fosters a sense of identity in which the true self sees itself in a covenant of oneness—of a deep and abiding respect for all. This is ultimately how forces of prejudice of all kinds can be eventually overcome. The shared responsibility of addressing the disease of racism becomes paramount, even while different individuals and groups have different roles to play in its eradication. Bahá'ís remain acutely aware that overcoming the devastating effects of racism, requires conscious, deliberate, and sustained effort by all. Indeed, "nothing short of genuine love, extreme patience, true humility" and "prayerful"

6. The Universal House of Justice, message addressed to the Bahá'ís of the United States, dated 22 July 2020.

reflection will succeed in effacing its pernicious stain from daily life. Thus, no real change will come about without close association, fellowship, and sincere friendship among diverse people. *"Close your eyes to racial differences,"* is Bahá'u'lláh's counsel, *"and welcome all with the light of oneness."*[7]

Creating a just, united, and flourishing society in which all its members from all backgrounds and beliefs are empowered to contribute and uplift the entire social body, is the work of generations. But it is a task, fundamentally moral and spiritual in nature, that must be pursued. Bahá'u'lláh's assurance of the transformative power of justice provides a beacon for the way forward: "*Justice is a powerful force. It is, above all else, the conqueror of the citadels of the hearts and souls of men, and the revealer of the secrets of the world of being, and the standard-bearer of love and bounty.*"[8]

The hallmark of this work is building capacity for the application of spiritual principles to individual and collective life through processes of learning. Some elements of the foundational understanding that underlie these efforts are as follows:

Belief in a loving and all-powerful Creator, and the sense of purpose this can provide to human existence, gives us hope for the long-term fate of humanity growing toward unity and justice. We can observe a historical process through which human

7. Bahá'u'lláh, quoted in Shoghi Effendi, *The Advent of Divine Justice,* ¶55.
8. Bahá'u'lláh, *Epistle to the Son of the Wolf,* p. 31.

beings have gradually been able to function in collectivities of wider scope, from small bands to tribes to city-states to nations and international alliances. The world is faced now with both the capacity and the need to come together as one: The scientific and technological means are already there, and we face existential challenges that we can only solve if we work together as a species.

In this context, the destructive, disintegrative forces at work in the world can be seen alongside constructive and integrative forces as part of a larger process of change. Old social structures and patterns have to be dismantled to make room for new ones. This is a painful process, like birth pangs, but we can find hope in it, and we can choose to be part of movements toward integration and constructive change.

Faith in the intrinsic nobility of human beings, arising from the spiritual dimension of our reality, our souls, also gives us hope. This nobility has to be an object of education, thereby cultivating the moral capacity to overcome the kinds of promptings we also have toward othering, greed, and similar root sources of the problems we face. There is a relationship between the spiritual and moral growth of the individual and their efforts to serve and contribute to society. As we learn to cultivate our spiritual capacity, new kinds of power for change are released. Processes of education and training can awaken young and old to the spiritual principle of the oneness of humanity, and can generate knowledge, skills, attitudes, and spiritual qualities that enable us to work for the well-being of all. Cadres of social actors will need to be raised up, especially youth, for the work of rebuilding the essential structures of social life.

We are trying to create a reality that humanity has not seen before, which requires that we learn our way forward into the unknown. The process of change requires effort and learning on many fronts from intimate interactions at the grassroots to discourse on the national or international stage. To be effective, these different efforts need to be aligned within a conceptual framework that allows a shared understanding of spiritual principles, means and ends, approaches, learning objectives, and so on. Within such a shared, evolving framework, diverse experiences, understandings, and perspectives can come together and—through action, reflection, and learning over time—those involved can discern what is effective and how to move forward.

Barriers to shared well-being can be understood in terms of oppressive forms of power that are hoarded by the few and exercised on the many. There are other ways of conceiving of power, however, that offer scope for constructive agency: the power of love, the power of unity, the power of truth, the power of collective action, the power of sacrifice. Religion is a rich source of insight into these forms of power, and can inspire within the broader discourses of society the kind of moral awakening that is needed to overcome our challenges.

For examples of how these principles are being applied in practice through the widening embrace of the American and global Bahá'í community, we direct your attention to the list of resources offered at the end of this essay.

The Bahá'í Writings offer a hopeful vision of the future for America. 'Abdu'l-Bahá, the son of the Founder of the Faith, stated in a message to the American Bahá'í community: "*The continent of America is, in the eyes of the one true God, the land wherein the splendors of His light shall be revealed, where the mysteries of His Faith shall be unveiled, where the righteous will abide, and the free assemble.*"[9] To achieve its destiny, the nation and its inhabitants will have to purge themselves of certain attitudes and behaviors. Racism, a direct manifestation of a decidedly materialistic conception of human existence and purpose, is an illusion that has warped the nation's sense of reality and true identity. It can only be rooted out through a profound moral change: an animated understanding of humanity as one family. This understanding must transform our inner lives and social relationships, and shape our choices in the ordering of society, a process that will require action, reflection, perseverance, and, at times, sacrifice. Through the systematic process of developing, in a variety of social spaces, moral capabilities to effect such a transformation in both individual consciousness and the structure of social institutions, we can realize our ability to disable racism and every other instrument devised in this nation for one group to oppress another.

As we reflect on the formidable moral change necessary to see the elimination of racism in the United States, it is possible

9. 'Abdu'l-Bahá, *Tablets of the Divine Plan,* no. 9.2.

to be overcome with feelings of hopelessness. Guilt is another potential feeling when dealing with the question of morality, as one becomes focused on shortcomings. However, these feelings must be overcome with a sense of courage, faith, and confidence in others, so that all people see the potential in themselves to overcome division and prejudice. Courage and confidence must go hand in hand with humility, not to be confused with subservience, so self-confidence does not become arrogance or complacency.

Ultimately, any ability to commit to social transformation requires detachment and sacrifice. Whether it be patterns of thought, behavior and action, material comforts, opinion, or social status, sacrifice is letting go of that which is lower for the sake of something higher. On this theme, 'Abdu'l-Bahá offers the following analogy: "*If you plant a seed in the ground, a tree will become manifest from that seed. The seed sacrifices itself to the tree that will come from it. The seed is outwardly lost, destroyed; but the same seed which is sacrificed will be absorbed and embodied in the tree, its blossoms, fruit and branches. If the identity of that seed had not been sacrificed to the tree which became manifest from it, no branches, blossoms or fruits would have been forthcoming.*"[10]

It is through this process that the dark characteristics of a society raised with racism, and still grappling with it, will generate the qualities and attributes required of social transformation, to become a society illumined by oneness.

---

10. 'Abdu'l-Bahá, *The Promulgation of Universal Peace*, no. 133.8.

Resource List Documenting Bahá'í Experience in Contributing to the Elimination of Racism in America

Films

AN EXPANSIVE PROSPECT

https://www.bahai.org/video/expansive-prospect

An Expansive Prospect looks at four places in the world, capturing the efforts of individuals, communities, and institutions as they strive together to release the society-building power of the Bahá'í teachings in ever-greater measures. See the story about North Carolina at 38:40.

A RICH TAPESTRY

https://www.bahai.us/collection/a-rich-tapestry/

A Rich Tapestry is a video storytelling series that explores how people across the United States are putting love into action to build racially and culturally inclusive communities, showing real-world examples of cooperation, community building, and social-justice work.

Articles

THE BAHÁ'Í RESPONSE TO RACIAL INJUSTICE AND PURSUIT OF RACIAL UNITY, PARTS 1 & 2

Thomas, Richard. "The Bahá'í Response to Racial Injustice and Pursuit of Racial Unity, Part 1: 1912–1996," *The Bahá'í World: https://bahaiworld.bahai.org/library/the-bahai-response-to-racial-injustice-and-pursuit-of-racial-unity/*

Lample, Emily and Richard Thomas. "The Bahá'í Response to Racial Injustice and Pursuit of Racial Unity, Part 2: 1996–2021, *The Bahá'í World: https://bahaiworld.bahai.org/library/the-bahai-response-to-racial-injustice-and-pursuit-of-racial-unity-2/*

Together, these two articles trace the historical and contemporary efforts of the Bahá'í community in the United States to build enduring patterns of racial unity grounded in the spiritual principle of the oneness of humanity. They illustrate how Bahá'ís have moved from early acts of interracial fellowship to today's grassroots community-building processes that foster new social relationships, challenge prejudice, and contribute to long-term racial healing.

A NEW INSTITUTION OF LEARNING: THE TRAINING INSTITUTE

"A New Institution of Learning: The Training Institute: Elements of a Global Spiritual Endeavor (1996–2021)," *The Bahá'í World: https://bahaiworld.bahai.org/library/a-new-institution-of-learning-the-training-institute/*

The Bahá'í community is seeking to build a replicable system for building capacity for service within communities that empowers them to determine and pursue their aspirations.

EXPLORING A FRAMEWORK FOR THE ELIMINATION OF RACIAL PREJUDICE

Lample, Paul. "Exploring a Framework for the Elimination of Racial Prejudice," *The Journal of Bahá'í Studies,* 35.1–2, 2025.

A framework for eliminating racial prejudice in America is grounded in spiritual principles and community-building processes that address personal, social, and structural dimensions of racism. Through long-term collective learning, the cultivation of unity, and the development of capacities, relationships can be transformed and social norms reshaped.

RESPONDING TO INJUSTICE WITH CONSTRUCTIVE AGENCY

Smith, Derik and Michael Karlberg, "Responding to Injustice with Constructive Agency," in Robert Stockman (ed.), *The World of the Bahá'í Faith.* London: Routledge, 2022.

Social change can be achieved not through confrontation or protest, but through deliberate, non-adversarial building of new social structures and norms rooted in justice and solidarity.